Comprehension
Book 2

John Jackman

Using this book

This book will help you to develop your reading skills so that you understand and enjoy what you read even more. You will not only learn to read the lines, but to read between the lines and beyond them as well!

What's in a unit
Each unit is set out in the same way as the example here.

Unit heading
This tells you about the text you will be reading

Do you remember
Activities to practise and check your understanding

More to think about
Activities to practise and develop your understanding

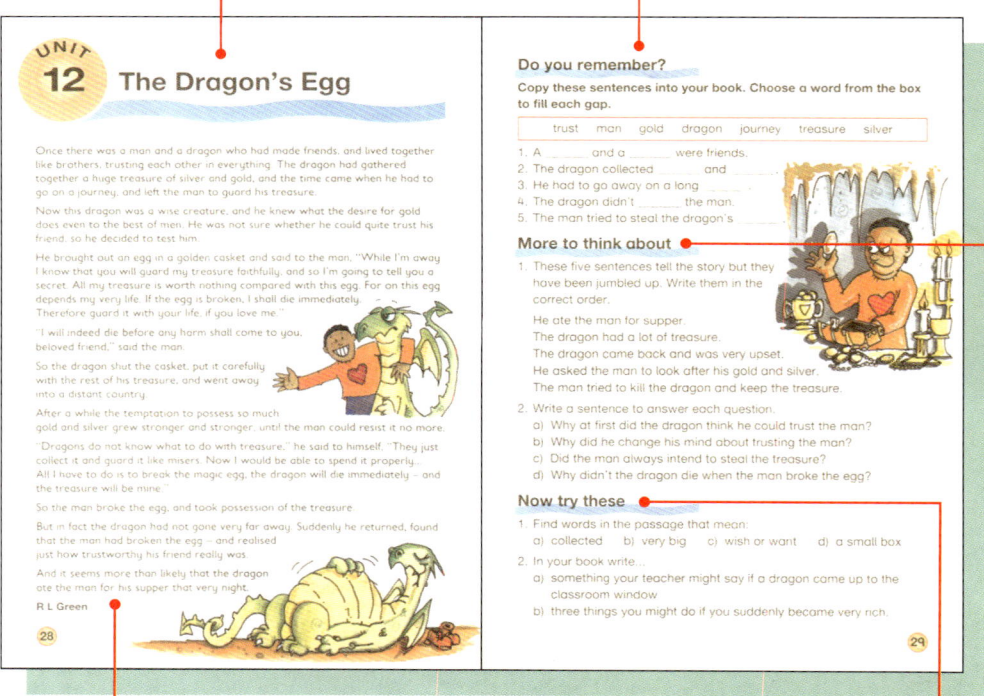

The text
The texts have been carefully selected to demonstrate all major genre types, from fiction to non-fiction

Now try these
Activities to stretch and extend your understanding

Contents

Unit		Page
1	The Eagle and the Turtle	4
2	On the Move	6
3	Growing	8
4	Three Girls	10
5	On Holiday	12
6	Magic	14
7	What's it all about?	16
8	Tim the Trumpet	18
9	The Wind in the Willows	20
10	I love our orange tent	22
Progress Unit A	The Accident	24
11	The Swoose	26
12	The Dragon's Egg	28
13	What is … the Sun?	30
14	Dr Xargle and the Earthlets	32
15	Feathered Record Breakers	34
16	Bus Route	36
17	A Day When Frogs Wear Shoes	38
18	Basilisks	40
19	Mrs Wobble the Waitress	42
20	Humans – friends or foes?	44
Progress Unit B	Being Angry	46

UNIT 1

The Eagle and the Turtle

A Turtle was not satisfied with his life. He wanted to stop being a Turtle. "I'm tired of swimming about in the sea and crawling about on the beach, getting nowhere in particular," he grumbled. "I want to be able to fly in the air like an eagle." He spoke to the Eagle about it. "You're not built for flying," the Eagle told the Turtle. "You haven't any wings." "Don't worry about that," answered the Turtle. "I've watched how the birds do it. I've watched them soar and glide, skim and dive. Even if I haven't got wings, I can make my four flippers act like four stout oars in the air, the way I do in the water. Just get me up there, and you'll see I can fly as well as any of the birds — probably better! Besides if you'll carry me as high as the clouds I'll bring you lots of rare pearls from the sea."

The Eagle was tempted, and carried the Turtle up to a great height. "Now, then," cried the Eagle, "fly!"

But the moment the Turtle was on his own, he fell from the sky. He fell like a stone, and on a stone he landed. He struck with such force that he smashed into little pieces.

Adapted from Aesop's Fables

Do you remember?

Copy these sentences. Fill in the missing words.
1. The Turtle wanted to be able to _____ in the sky.
2. He went to speak to the _____ about it.

3. The Eagle said he couldn't fly because he didn't have _____ .
4. The Turtle promised the Eagle rare _____ if he helped him.
5. When he tried to fly he fell like a _____ .

More to think about

1. Answer these questions in your book.
   a) What words does the Turtle use to describe how he would like to fly?
   b) What does he have that he thinks will help him to fly?
   c) How can we tell that the Eagle doesn't want to carry the Turtle high in the sky?
   d) How does the Turtle persuade the Eagle to help him?
   e) How does the writer describe how the Turtle fell?

2. Write the story in your own words in a short form. Try to use no more than three sentences.

Now try these

1. Make up a good ending for each of these sentences. Write the complete sentences in your book.
   a) The Turtle was not satisfied with his life because….
   b) He thought that if only he could fly he would be able to….
   c) The Eagle really didn't want to carry the Turtle into the sky because….

2. a) Write two good things and two bad things about being a turtle.
   b) Write two good things and two bad things about being an eagle.

3. There are two 'morals' to this fable:

   Be satisfied with what you are.

   The higher you fly, the harder you may fall.

   Write in your own words what each means.

UNIT 2
On the Move

Planes, ships, trains, cars and buses carry people and freight from one place to another. The way people and things are moved depends on how quickly they need to travel, and where they are going.

A container ship can carry more than the aeroplane, but is much slower.

Trains can carry far more than trucks, but trucks are still needed to collect the goods from the train at the end of its journey.

Buses and coaches carry more people than cars, but don't usually take you to the final destination, so most people prefer to go places by car if they have one.

Do you remember?

Copy these sentences. Choose the correct word. The sentences and diagram will help you.
1. An oil tanker carries _____. (oil **or** tanks)
2. Aeroplanes are _____ than ships. (slower **or** faster)
3. Trucks can carry _____ than trains. (more **or** less)
4. Buses and coaches carry _____. (people **or** freight)
5. Most people prefer to travel by _____. (bus **or** car)

More to think about

1. List the things in this picture:
    a) that carry freight
    b) that carry people.

2. What would be the best way to:
    a) move food from a factory to the shops?
    b) get your class to the local swimming pool?
    c) bring oil from 2000 kilometres away?
    d) get to Spain on holiday?
    e) move large amounts of coal to a power station?

Now try these

1. Write sentences to answer these questions.
    a) Why do people usually like to travel by car if they have one?
    b) What problems can there be about travelling by car?
    c) Why is it better if more goods can be sent by train?
    d) Do you think more people should travel by bike? Give your reasons.
2. Write a letter to your Member of Parliament giving all the reasons why a new airport should not be built in fields near to your house.

UNIT 3 Growing

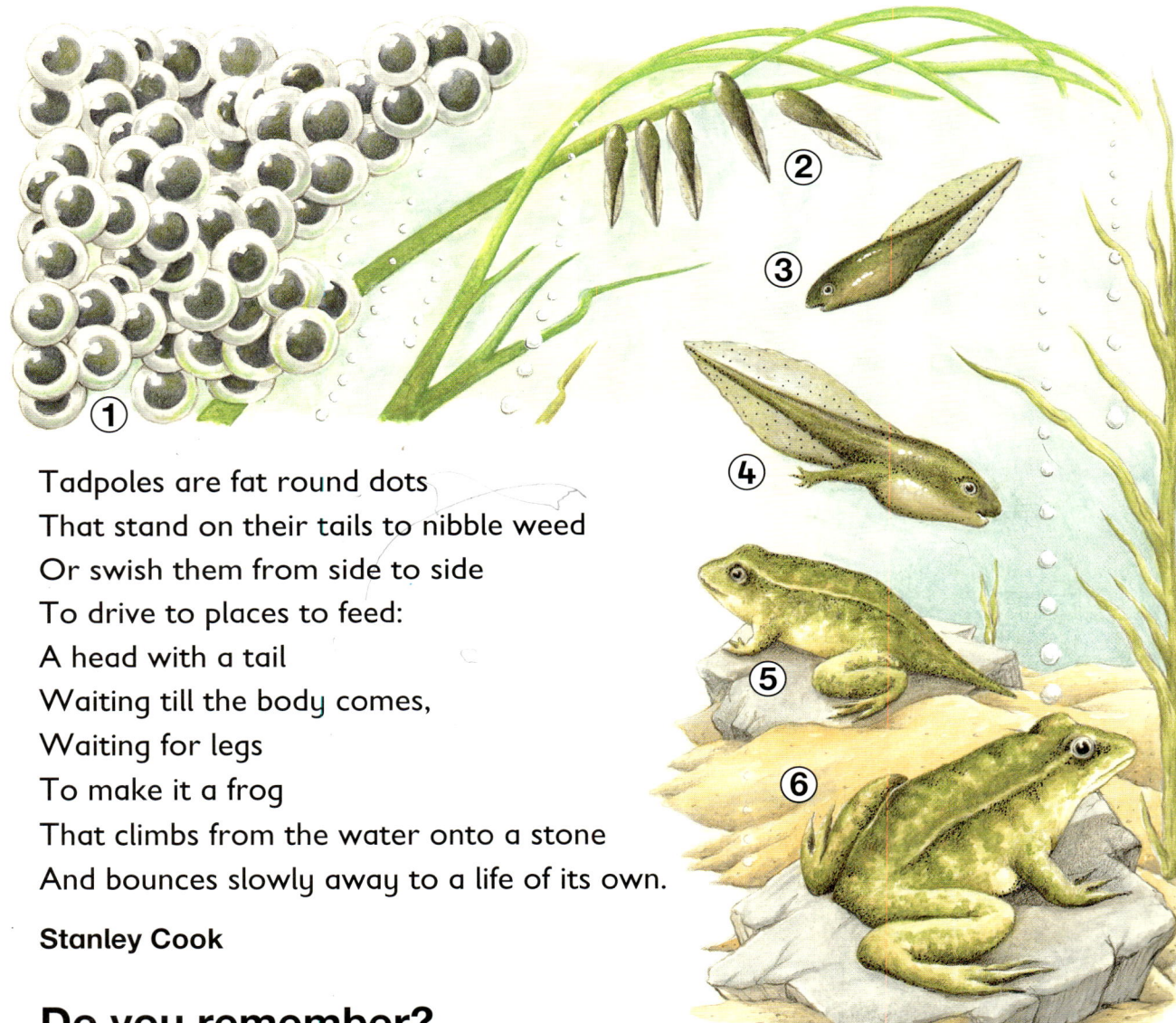

Tadpoles are fat round dots
That stand on their tails to nibble weed
Or swish them from side to side
To drive to places to feed:
A head with a tail
Waiting till the body comes,
Waiting for legs
To make it a frog
That climbs from the water onto a stone
And bounces slowly away to a life of its own.

Stanley Cook

Do you remember?

**Read the poem and look carefully at the pictures.
Copy the lines from the poem…**
1. …that most closely match picture number 1
2. …that most closely match picture number 2
3. …that most closely match picture number 4

More to think about

1. These sentences about tadpoles are from an information book.
   They have been muddled up. Write them in the correct order.

   > Their tails get shorter, and disappear.
   > Little tadpoles grow inside the jelly.
   > Soon their rear legs begin to grow.
   > The tadpoles hatch from the jelly.
   > The tadpoles have become frogs.
   > The frog lays her eggs, called frogspawn.

2. Imagine that you are writing an information book.
   Write some sentences to describe the order of what happens from the time you buy some bulbs until you have some beautiful flowers.

Now try these

1. In the fairy story the prince was turned into a frog.
   Pretend you were the prince.
   Write about how it felt not being able to tell anyone that you were not really a frog, but a person.

2. Tell the story of some scary or funny things that happened to you.

UNIT 4

Three Girls

There were three girls and they were going for a walk along the beach until they came to a cave.
One of the girls says, "I'm going in."
So she goes in.

When she gets in, she sees a pile of gold sitting on the rocks, so she thinks, "Yippee, gold, all for me!" and she steps forward to pick it up and a great big voice booms out, "I'm the ghost of Captain Cox. All the gold stays on the rocks."

So the girl runs out of the cave.

The second girl goes in and she sees the gold and she thinks, "Yippee, gold, all for me!" and she steps forward to pick it up and the great big voice booms out, "I'm the ghost of Captain Cox. All the gold stays on the rocks."

So the girl runs out of the cave.

Then the third girl goes in and she sees the gold and she thinks, "Yippee, gold, all for me!" and she steps forward to pick it up and the great big voice booms out, "I'm the ghost of Captain Cox. All the gold stays on the rocks."

And the girl says,
"I don't care. I'm the ghost of Davy Crocket and all the gold stays in my pocket!"
And she runs out of the cave with the gold.

Michael Rosen

Do you remember?

Write the correct answer to each question in your book.
1. Are there three girls walking along the beach?
   a) No, there are four girls walking along the beach.
   b) Yes, there are three girls walking along the beach.
2. What did the girls come to?
   a) They came to a cave.   b) They came to a lighthouse.
3. What is inside the cave?
   a) There is a boat in the cave.   b) There is gold in the cave.
4. Why do the first and second girls run out of the cave?
   a) They are frightened by a big animal.
   b) They are frightened by a ghost.
5. Is the third girl brave enough to enter the cave?
   a) Yes, the third girl goes into the cave.
   b) No, the third girl doesn't go into the cave.

More to think about

1. Write a sentence to answer each question.
   a) Did the first girl plan to share the gold with her friends?
   b) How might the gold have come to be in the cave?
   c) Why might the ghost of Captain Cox think the gold was his?
   d) Was the ghost successful in protecting the gold?

2. Write the story in your own words. Don't use more than 40 words.

Now try these

1. Make a list of all the dangers there could be in a cave.

2. Write in your book how you would have felt if:
   a) you had been the first girl   b) you had been the third girl

3. In your book, write what is being said.

4. Find a word in the poem to rhyme with: a) Cox   b) Crocket

UNIT 5 On Holiday

Here are instructions we found in our holiday apartment.

Sandy Bay Holiday Park

Welcome to Sandy Bay Holiday Park. We hope you will enjoy your stay with us.

To help you find your feet as quickly as possible, may we offer some advice.

1. Walk around the park to get your bearings.
2. Visit our supermarket to stock up with provisions.
3. Come to the bar for your welcome drink, with the compliments of the management.

We don't have many rules, but those we do are to ensure you and other guests enjoy a relaxed holiday, away from the hurly-burly of everyday life!

Rule 1: Please return to the park no later than 11.30 pm.
Rule 2: No noise outside your caravan after midnight.
Rule 3: No loud music at any time.
Rule 4: Swimming pool not to be used by unaccompanied children under 7 years at any time.
Rule 5: No swimming in pool after 9 pm.

Have a great holiday!

We were also given this map.

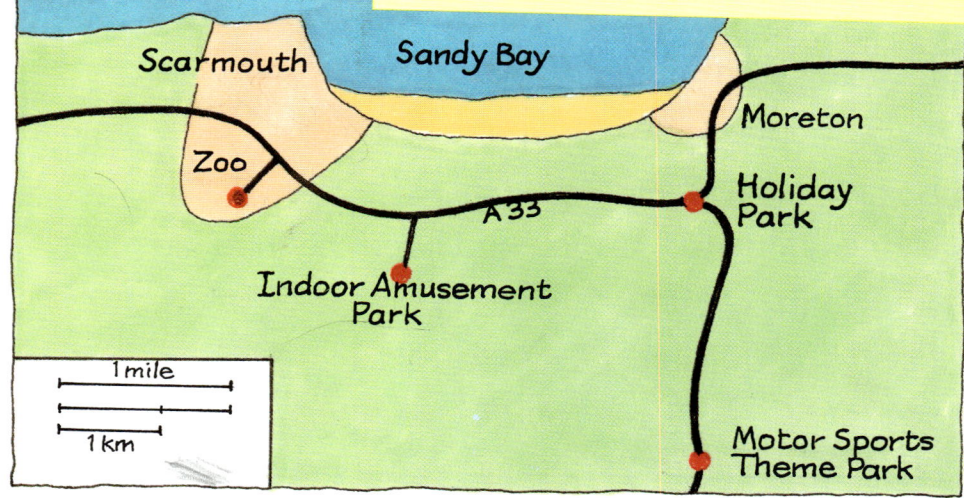

Do you remember?

Copy these sentences. Fill in the missing words.
1. Our family went to _____ for our holiday.
2. When we arrived we were given instructions and a _____.
3. The instructions suggested the first thing to do was _____ around the park.
4. When we went to the bar they gave us a free _____.
5. Nobody was allowed in the swimming pool after _____.

More to think about

1. Write a sentence to answer each question.
   a) How far is it to the beach?
   b) What is the nearest town?
   c) Is the Motor Sports theme park close enough to walk to?
   d) Where is the zoo?
   e) What might be the best thing for the family to do when it rains?

2. What do each of these phrases mean?
   a) help you find your feet
   b) to stock up with provisions
   c) with the compliments of the management
   d) away from the hurly-burly of everyday life
   e) unaccompanied children

Now try these

Write sentences in your book to answer these questions.
1. What reasons could the management have for suggesting that one of the first things to do is to go to the supermarket?
2. Why would they ask that everyone has returned to the park by 11.30 pm?
3. Do you agree that children under 7 years should not be allowed to swim without an adult?
4. If you were the manager of the holiday park, what rules would you make? Write them out neatly.

Magic

Sandra's seen a leprechaun,
Eddie touched a troll,
Laurie danced with witches once,
Charlie found some goblin's gold.
Donald heard a mermaid sing,
Susie spied an elf,
But all the magic I have known
I've had to make myself.

Shel Silverstein

Do you remember?

Match these questions and answers.
Write them in your book, like this:

What did Sandra see?   She saw a leprechaun.

What did Sandra see?	He touched a troll.
Who danced with the witches?	A mermaid was singing.
What did Charlie find?	She saw a leprechaun.
Who was singing?	Laurie danced with them.
What did Eddie touch?	He found some goblin's gold.

More to think about

From what it says in the poem, write in your book 'true', 'false', or 'can't tell' for each of these sentences.

1. Sandra likes leprechauns.
2. Eddie has seen a troll.
3. Witches can dance.
4. Laurie often dances with witches.
5. The goblin's gold was hidden in a cave.
6. Mermaids only sing sea-shanties.
7. Susie talked to an elf.
8. The elf was in Susie's garden.

Now try these

1. In your book write:
    a) something your teacher might say when she finds a goblin under her table
    b) something your mum might say when you bring a witch home to tea
    c) something your friend might say when you explain about a family of elves that you have seen under a bush on your way to school.

2. What does the poet mean when he says:
    'But all the magic I have known
    I've had to make myself'?

UNIT 7 What's it all about?

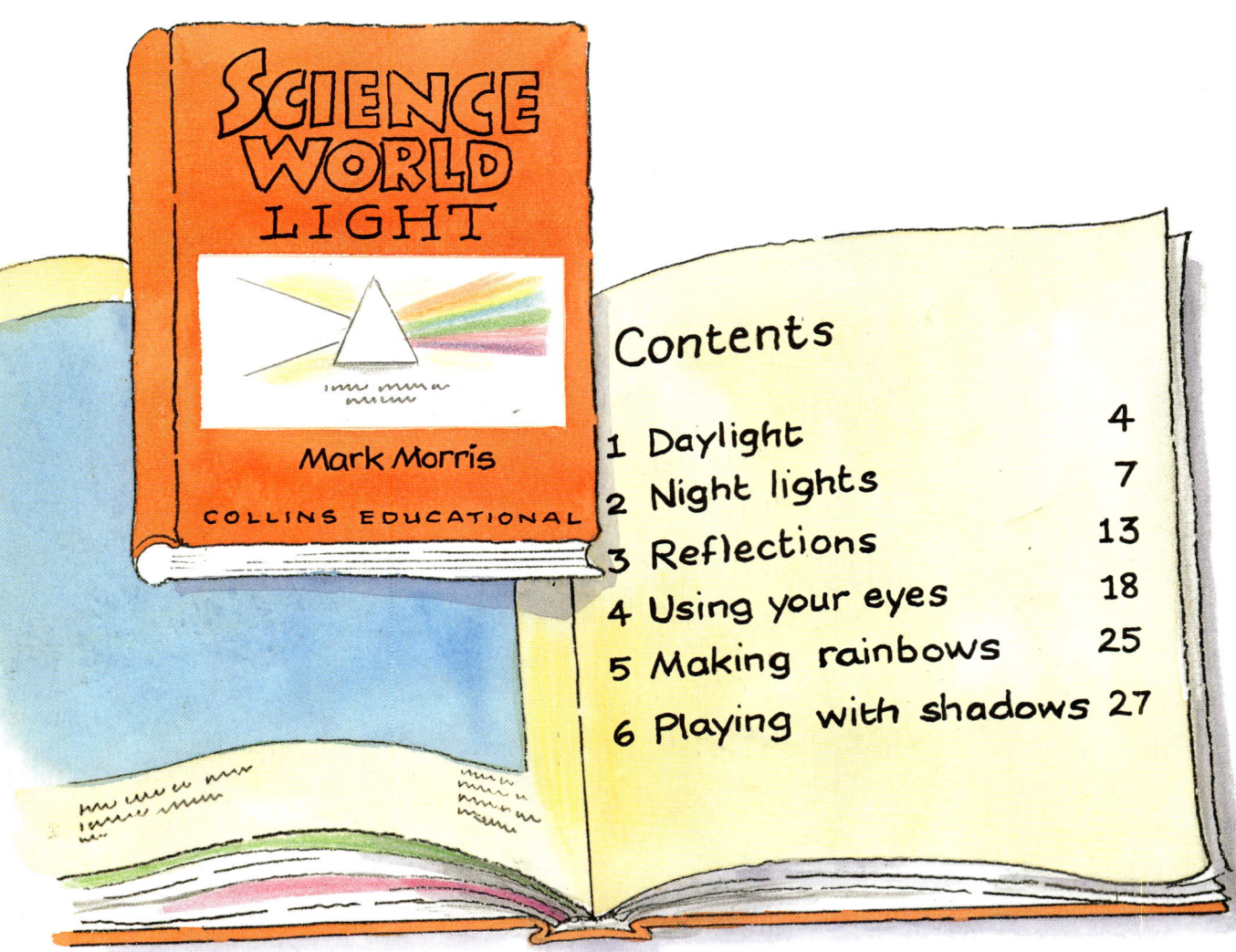

Do you remember?

Copy these sentences. Fill in the missing words.
1. The book is in a series called _____ World.
2. The title of the book is _____.
3. It is written by _____ _____.
4. The first chapter is called _____.
5. The last chapter is about _____.

More to think about

Answer these quick questions with a word or a number.
1. What is chapter 3 about?
2. In which chapter can I read about rainbows?
3. How many chapters are there in the book?
4. On which page can I begin to read about eyes?
5. How many pages are there in chapter 5?
6. How many pages are there in chapter 2?
7. In which chapter might I find out about the moon?
8. In which chapter might I find out about mirrors?
9. Write the title of another book that you might expect to find in this series.
10. What is the name of the publisher of the book?

Now try these

Find in your library *two* books which interest you. Answer these questions for each one.
1. What is the title of the book?
2. Who is the author?
3. What is the name of the publisher?
4. What is the book about?
5. How many chapters are in the book?
6. How many pages are in the book?
7. On which page does the first chapter begin?
8. On which page does chapter 3 begin?
9. What is the title of the second chapter?
10. What do you most like about the book?

UNIT 8

Tim the Trumpet

To look at, Tim was a perfectly ordinary boy. His hair stood on end and his face was never quite clean. His jeans were definitely dusty and his T-shirt always managed to be back to front. But all this could happen to anyone. What made Tim quite different from anybody else was his voice.

Tim's voice was truly amazing. It was like a cross between a factory hooter and a foghorn. Or perhaps a roll of thunder and a ship's siren. And there was nothing he could do about it. It was just something he had been born with. His parents, of course, noticed his voice right from the start.

When Tim was a baby he would, like any other baby, let out a cry to tell everyone that he wasn't happy. Only it wasn't so much a cry, it was more like – well – an alarm bell going off. It certainly alarmed the neighbours. They used to gather in the street outside the house, and discuss in worried whispers whether they ought to call the police. They were certain something terrible was happening!

Tim's parents had to explain... "It's his voice you see. Tim has this very, very loud voice..."

Even so, when Tim was christened, the Vicar – who had been warned beforehand – wisely wore ear muffs.

Elisabeth Beresford

Do you remember?

What words are missing from the passage?

__1__ seemed a very ordinary boy. His face was never quite __2__ and he wore his __3__ back to front. He had a very loud __4__. He had had it since he was a __5__. It worried the __6__. They thought they should call the __7__. When Tim was christened the __8__ wore ear muffs.

18

More to think about

Write sentences to answer these questions.
1. In the story Tim's voice is described as being like other loud noises.
   a) What was it like when he was a baby?
   b) What noises was it like when he got older?
2. Describe what Tim usually looked like.
3. Why did the neighbours think they should call the police?
4. Did Tim make loud noises because his parents were unkind to him?
5. How did the Vicar know he should wear ear muffs?

Now try these

1. Sometimes we say things are **like**, or **similar to**, other things. When we do this we are using **similes**. Similes often begin with **like** or **as**. Copy these sentences, and neatly underline the similes. The first is done to help you.
   a) Tim's voice was <u>like a foghorn</u>.
   b) Tim's mother thought her baby was as pretty as a picture.
   c) Some people said Tim's voice was like a ship's siren.
   d) When Tim was a baby he sounded as loud as an alarm bell.
   e) When Tim was older he could call across the playground as easy as pie.

2. Which creature do you think of to finish these similes?

   a) as brave as a _____
   b) as cunning as a _____
   c) as timid as a _____
   d) as quiet as a _____
   e) as fast as a _____
   f) as happy as a _____
   g) as slow as a _____
   h) as obstinate as a _____
   i) as slippery as an _____
   j) as wise as an _____

   The names in the box might help you, but you can also think of your own similes.

   | fox   hare   lark   eel   owl   tortoise   mule   rabbit   mouse   lion |

The Wind in the Willows

The Mole, who had been busily spring-cleaning his house, had come out for a rest...

As he sat on the grass and looked across the river, a dark hole in the bank opposite, just above the water's edge, caught his eye. Something bright and small seemed to twinkle down in the heart of it, vanish, then twinkle once more like a tiny star. But it could hardly be a star in such an unlikely situation, and it was too glittering and small for a glow-worm. Then, as he looked, it winked at him, and so declared itself to be an eye, and a small face began gradually to grow up round it, like a frame round a picture.

A brown little face, with whiskers.
A grave round face, with the same twinkle in its eye that had first attracted his notice.
Small neat ears and thick silky hair.
It was the Water Rat!

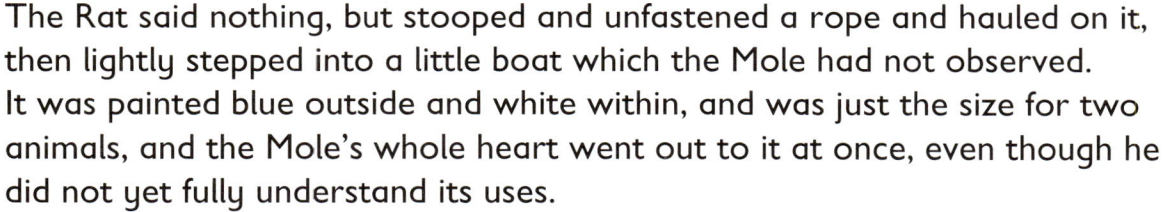

The Rat said nothing, but stooped and unfastened a rope and hauled on it, then lightly stepped into a little boat which the Mole had not observed. It was painted blue outside and white within, and was just the size for two animals, and the Mole's whole heart went out to it at once, even though he did not yet fully understand its uses.

The Rat sculled smartly across and made fast. Then he held up his fore-paw as the Mole stepped gingerly down. "Lean on that!" he said. "Now then, step lively!" and the Mole to his surprise and rapture found himself actually seated in the stern of a real boat.

"This has been a wonderful day!" said he, as the Rat shoved off and took to the sculls again. "Do you know, I've never been in a boat before in all my life."

Kenneth Grahame

Do you remember?

Read these sentences about the story.
Copy only the ones that are true.
1. Mole lived by the river.
2. He saw a glow-worm.
3. He could see the Water Rat on the opposite bank.
4. The Rat swam across the river to see him.
5. The Rat had a boat.
6. The boat was painted blue and white.

More to think about

1. Write a sentence to answer each question.
   a) How did Mole know the twinkle he saw on the opposite bank was not a star?
   b) Was Rat's boat large or small?
   c) What words tell us that Mole was excited when he first saw the boat?
   d) Why was Mole rather unsure about getting into Rat's boat?

2. Choose groups of words from each column to make sensible sentences. Copy the correct sentences into your book.

Who?	Did what?	Where?
The Mole	came out of	across the river.
The Rat	sat	his hole.
The Rat	sculled	on the grass.

Now try these

1. What words does the author use:
   a) to describe Rat's face?
   b) to describe how Rat brought the boat across the river?
   c) to describe how Mole got into the boat?

2. Think back to when you did something for the first time, and describe your feelings. Were you frightened or excited, or a bit of both? What other feelings did you have?

UNIT 10   I love our orange tent

I love our orange tent.
We plant it like a flower
in the field.
The grass smells sweet inside it.

    And at night
    When we're lying in it,
    I hear the owl crying.

        When the wind blows,
        my tent flaps
        like a flying bird.

            And the rain
            patters down on it
            with tiny footsteps.

                I feel warm and safe
                inside my tent.

                    But when the sun shines,
                    that's when I love it best!

                        When I wake up
                        and the sun is shining,
                        it pours in like yellow honey.
                        It glows like gold.

                            I love our orange tent.

                        Berlie Doherty

Do you remember?

Copy these sentences. Fill in the missing words.
1. The children love their orange _____.
2. They put it up in the _____.
3. At night they can hear the _____ crying.
4. When the wind blows, the tent _____.
5. They like being in the tent best when the sun is _____.

More to think about

Write a sentence to answer each question.
1. Why does the poet say that they plant the tent like a flower in the field?
2. Does she like the smell of the grass in the orange tent?
3. What does the tent sound like when the wind blows?
4. Do you think the fourth verse describes heavy rain or light rain? Give your reasons.
5. Why does the poet like being in the tent most when the sun shines?

Now try these

Imagine that the orange tent is your tent.
1. What do you think are the best things about going camping? Make a list.
2. Now make a list of all the problems that could happen on a camping trip.

Progress Unit A

The Accident

Second ice fatality in a week

Tragedy struck again yesterday when an elderly lady fell through the ice. Mrs Wills, 79, of Onslow Gardens had been walking alone with her sister's dog when it chased a duck onto the frozen river. It is the first time in living memory that the River Thames has frozen from bank to bank.

Onlookers struggled desperately to save Mrs Wills when she fell through the ice whilst trying to rescue the black labrador. Rescue Services were on the scene within five minutes, but as Chief Officer Chung said, "There was no way anyone could survive more than a minute or two in water with sub-zero temperatures."

Last week the same rescue crew tried unsuccessfully to rescue an eight year old boy who had been playing on the ice.

Do you remember?

Read these sentences about the newspaper report.
Write in your book 'true', 'false', or 'can't tell' for each one.

1. Mrs Wills had been walking with her husband.
2. She was wearing a red coat and blue scarf.
3. It was very unusual for the River Thames to freeze right across.
4. There was nobody around to help Mrs Wills.
5. The dog managed to scramble to safety.

More to think about

1. Here are the **answers** to five questions about the newspaper article. Write in your book what the questions must have been.
   The first has been done to help you.
   a) Mrs Wills was 79.   How old was Mrs Wills?
   b) She went onto the ice to rescue the dog.
   c) It was a black labrador dog.
   d) The Rescue Services arrived within five minutes.
   e) Last week they tried to save an eight year old boy.

2. The newspaper editor has said the article is too long.
   Re-write the article in your own words in no more than 60 words.

Now try these

1. Make two lists, one with the good things about winter and another with the bad things about winter. Try to think of other people and creatures, as well as yourself.

2. Imagine that you were walking along the bank of the river just as the dog went onto the ice. You could see the possible danger ahead for the old lady. Write about what you would have done, without putting yourself in danger.

3. Write sentences of your own to show that you know what each of these words mean:
   a) fatality   b) tragedy   c) elderly   d) desperately

UNIT 11 The Swoose

Fitzherbert was aware that he looked different from the other goslings on the farm. One day his goose mother explained....

She lowered her voice.
"You," she said softly, "are a swoose."
Fitzherbert coiled his long neck backwards into the shape of an S.
"A what?" he cried.
"Sssssssh!" hissed his mother, and she waddled off to a distant corner of the farmyard, away from all the other geese. Fitzherbert hurried after her.
"What did you say I was?" he asked.
His mother looked around to make sure they were out of earshot of the rest of the flock, and then she said, "Now listen carefully. What I am about to tell you must be a secret between you and me, always. D'you understand?"
"Yes, Mum," said Fitzherbert.
"You are old enough now to be told," said his mother, "why you are unlike all the other goslings on the farm. They are the children of a number of geese, but they all have the same father."
"The old grey gander, you mean?"
"Yes."
"But isn't he my father too?"
"No."
"Then who is?"
"Your father," said Fitzherbert's mum, and a dreamy look came over her face as she spoke, "is neither old nor grey. Your father is young and strong and as white as the driven snow."

Dick King-Smith

Do you remember?

**Choose the right answer for each question.
Write the answers in your book.**
1. Fitzherbert's mother was
   a) a swan   b) a duck   c) a goose
2. Fitzherbert thought he was
   a) a swan   b) a duck   c) a goose
3. He had always thought his father was
   a) the old grey gander   b) a cockerel   c) a white swan
4. His mother told him about his father
   a) in a corner of the farmyard   b) in the barn   c) behind a shed
5. His mother told Fitzherbert that his father was
   a) the old grey gander   b) a cockerel   c) a white swan

More to think about

1. Write a sentence to answer each question.
   a) What clue does the author give us near the beginning that Fitzherbert might be related to a swan?
   b) Why did his mother want to tell him away from the other geese?
   c) What words does the author use to show that Fitzherbert's mother was very fond of his real father?

2. If a swoose has a swan father and a goose mother, write the name for a creature which is a cross between:
   a) a shark and a whale   b) a bat and a robin   c) a pig and a cow
   Choose one and describe its looks and unusual ways.

Now try these

1. What do the following phrases mean?
   a) lowered her voice   b) out of earshot   c) white as the driven snow
2. If you were the swoose, describe how you would feel when your mother gave you the surprise news about your father.
3. This is the beginning of a story. Write a few sentences to tell how, if you were the author, you would finish the story of the swoose.

UNIT 12 The Dragon's Egg

Once there was a man and a dragon who had made friends, and lived together like brothers, trusting each other in everything. The dragon had gathered together a huge treasure of silver and gold, and the time came when he had to go on a journey, and left the man to guard his treasure.

Now this dragon was a wise creature, and he knew what the desire for gold does even to the best of men. He was not sure whether he could quite trust his friend, so he decided to test him.

He brought out an egg in a golden casket and said to the man, "While I'm away I know that you will guard my treasure faithfully, and so I'm going to tell you a secret. All my treasure is worth nothing compared with this egg. For on this egg depends my very life. If the egg is broken, I shall die immediately. Therefore guard it with your life, if you love me."

"I will indeed die before any harm shall come to you, beloved friend," said the man.

So the dragon shut the casket, put it carefully with the rest of his treasure, and went away into a distant country.

After a while the temptation to possess so much gold and silver grew stronger and stronger, until the man could resist it no more.

"Dragons do not know what to do with treasure," he said to himself. "They just collect it and guard it like misers. Now I would be able to spend it properly... All I have to do is to break the magic egg, the dragon will die immediately – and the treasure will be mine."

So the man broke the egg, and took possession of the treasure.

But in fact the dragon had not gone very far away. Suddenly he returned, found that the man had broken the egg – and realised just how trustworthy his friend really was.

And it seems more than likely that the dragon ate the man for his supper that very night.

R L Green

Do you remember?

Copy these sentences into your book. Choose a word from the box to fill each gap.

> trust   man   gold   dragon   journey   treasure   silver

1. A _____ and a _____ were friends.
2. The dragon collected _____ and _____ .
3. He had to go away on a long _____ .
4. The dragon didn't _____ the man.
5. The man tried to steal the dragon's _____ .

More to think about

1. These five sentences tell the story but they have been jumbled up. Write them in the correct order.

   He ate the man for supper.
   The dragon had a lot of treasure.
   The dragon came back and was very upset.
   He asked the man to look after his gold and silver.
   The man tried to kill the dragon and keep the treasure.

2. Write a sentence to answer each question.
   a) Why at first did the dragon think he could trust the man?
   b) Why did he change his mind about trusting the man?
   c) Did the man always intend to steal the treasure?
   d) Why didn't the dragon die when the man broke the egg?

Now try these

1. Find words in the passage that mean:
   a) collected   b) very big   c) wish or want   d) a small box

2. In your book write...
   a) something your teacher might say if a dragon came up to the classroom window
   b) three things you might do if you suddenly became very rich.

UNIT 13 What is ... the Sun?

The Sun is a star. It is the nearest star to Earth, which is why it seems much bigger than any other star, but really the Sun is quite a small star. Some stars, that are much further away, are thousands of times bigger than the Sun.

The sun is a huge ball of fiery gas. It is 150 million kilometres from Earth, and without it there would be no light or warmth on Earth. If the Sun did not give us light and heat there would be no life on Earth, so the Sun is very important to us. We are not its only planet, though; it has eight others.

It takes Earth about 365 days, or one year, to travel once round the Sun.

Here is the way a poet sees the Sun.

> The sun is an orange dinghy
>   sailing across a calm sea.
>
> It is a gold coin
>   dropped down a drain in heaven.
>
> It is a yellow beach ball
>   kicked high into the summer sky.
>
> It is a red thumb-print
>   on a sheet of pale blue paper.
>
> It is the gold top from a milk bottle
>   floating on a puddle.

Wes Magee

Do you remember?

Copy these sentences. Choose the right ending.

1. Most stars are — smaller than the sun.
   — the same size as the Sun.
   — bigger than the Sun.

2. The Sun is made of — glowing rocks. / red water. / fiery gases.

3. From Earth to the Sun is — 15 million kilometres. / 150 million kilometres. / 1500 million kilometres.

4. Once every year — the Sun travels around the Earth. / the Moon travels around the Earth. / the Earth travels around the Sun.

More to think about

1. Use the grid to answer the questions. The first one is done to help you.

	A	B	C
1	150	light	8
2	heat	365	the Sun
3	1	gas	thousands

   a) How many planets, apart from Earth, does the Sun have?   C1
   b) How many times bigger than the Sun are some other stars?
   c) What two important things does the Sun gives to Earth?
   d) How many days does the Earth take to circle the Sun?
   e) How many years does the Earth take to circle the Sun?
   f) Which is the nearest star to Earth?
   g) What is the Sun made of?

2. The poet cleverly compares the Sun with other things.
   a) What is 'the calm sea' in the first verse?
   b) Where does the poet think heaven is, in the second verse?
   c) What is the 'sheet of pale blue paper', in the fourth verse?
   d) Which verse do you like best? Why?

Now try these

Poets often compare things. Write down three things which remind you of each of these.

1. The sea   2. A snake   3. An ant's nest

UNIT 14

Dr Xargle and the Earthlets

A teacher on an unknown planet, billions and trillions of miles away, is giving her class a geography lesson.

Today we are going to learn about Earthlets. They come in four colours. Pink, brown, black or yellow... but not green.
They have one head and only two eyes, two short tentacles with pheelers on the end and two long tentacles called leggies. They have square claws which they use to frighten off wild beasts known as Tibbles and Marmaduke. Earthlets grow fur on their heads but not enough to keep them warm.

Earthlets have no fangs at birth.
For many days they drink only milk through a hole in their face. When they have finished the milk they must be patted and squeezed to stop them exploding.
When they grow a fang, the parent Earthling takes the egg of a hen and mangles it with a prong. Then she puts the eggmangle on a small spade and tips it into the Earthlet's mouth, nose and ears.

Earthlets can be recognised by their fierce cry, "WAAAAAAA!"
To stop them doing this, the Earthlet daddy picks them up and flings them into the atmosphere.

If they still cry they are sent to a place called beddybyes.

Jeanne Willis

Do you remember?

Copy these sentences. Choose the correct words to fill the gaps.
1. The teacher is giving a lesson about _____ .   (Starlets **or** Earthlets)
2. Earthlets are never _____ .   (green **or** pink)
3. They grow fur on their _____ .   (legs **or** heads)
4. They are patted to stop them _____ .   (crying **or** exploding)
5. If they still cry they are sent to _____ .   (beddybyes **or** the garden)

More to think about

1. Write a sentence to answer each question.
    a) What is an Earthlet?
    b) On which planet do they live?
    c) What are the 'two short tentacles with pheelers on the end'?
    d) Who or what are 'Tibbles and Marmaduke'?
    e) What do we call 'eggmangle on a small spade'?

2. Use the clues in the passage to answer these questions about the 'unknown planet billions and trillions of miles away'.
    a) What colour are the people who live there?
    b) Do they have more than or fewer than two eyes?
    c) What keeps these strange people warm?
    d) Would you expect them to have large teeth?
    e) Would you expect to find other creatures on their planet?

Now try these

Imagine that your spacecraft has just secretly visited Planet Earth from this unknown planet. Choose one of these things you have been watching, and write in your book how you will explain it to people when you return to your own planet.
   a) a cricket match   b) a railway train
   c) a beach in summer   d) a classroom

UNIT 15 Feathered Record Breakers

Here is a page from a reference book about birds.

Biggest alive
The giant of the bird world is the ostrich, from Africa. It grows up to 2.7 metres and can weigh over 155 kilograms. Its eggs are also the biggest, weighing in at 1.5 kilograms.

Heaviest extinct bird
The roc, or elephant bird, lived in Madagascar until 300 years ago. It weighed over 420 kilograms, and laid eggs 7 times as big as the ostrich.

Heaviest flier
The African kori bustard has been known to weigh 18 kilograms.

Tallest extinct bird
Some species of the New Zealand moa grew to over 4 metres, but they died out about 700 years ago.

Fastest flier
Spine-tailed swifts can reach 170 kilometres per hour.

Fastest runner
Ostriches can run at 65 kph.

Greatest wingspan
The wandering albatross has a wingspan up to 3 metres.

Smallest bird
The bee hummingbird measures less than 6 centimetres from beak to tail and weighs 2 grams.

Deepest divers
Emperor penguins have been known to reach depths of over 250 metres.

Do you remember?

Write a sentence to answer each question.
1. Where are ostriches found in the wild?
2. How fast can the spine-tailed swift fly?
3. Which bird has the widest wingspan?

4. How long is a bee hummingbird from beak to tail?
5. Which birds have dived to 250 metres?

More to think about

From what it tells us on the page from the reference book, write in your book 'true', 'false', or 'can't tell' for each of these statements.

1. Ostriches are the biggest birds ever to have lived.
2. Ostriches are bigger than emus.
3. Emperor penguins can't live in shallow water.
4. Albatrosses can fly faster than buzzards.
5. Bee hummingbirds only live in jungles.
6. An ostrich's egg is bigger than that of the African kori bustard.
7. The tallest person who ever lived was 2 metres 72 centimetres, more than a metre shorter than the extinct New Zealand moa.
8. Cheetahs can run at 100 kilometres per hour, which is faster than the fastest bird can run.
9. Cheetahs are able to run faster than any bird can fly.
10. London Zoo has a breeding pair of elephant birds.

Now try these

1. Imagine that you could be a record breaker. Write some sentences about which records you would like to break, and say why.

2. These words all describe size.

| large   colossal   dwarf   massive   wee   little   midget   bulky |
| miniature   great   mini   minute   tiny   enormous   mighty   huge |

a) Use a dictionary to help you sort them into two lists, like this:

Words meaning big	Words meaning small

b) Take a word from each list and write each one in a sentence to show that you know what they mean.

UNIT 16 Bus Route

When the bus is full
it creeps uphill
like an old man climbing
the stairs to bed.

Down the other side
it rumbles into town
barging through the traffic,
an angry bully.

Out in the country
the bus is empty
rattling through the quiet lanes
humming softly.

But it can never stay;
it has to push and shove,
bruise and scrape its skin
in the rough and tumble town.

Surging crowds of people
swarm and clamber on it,
fill it to the top
at the bottom of the hill.

David Harmer

Do you remember?

Copy these sentences. Choose the correct words to fill the gaps.
1. The bus starts at the _____ of the hill.   (top **or** bottom)
2. First it is going into the _____.   (town **or** country)
3. In town the bus has to barge through the _____.   (people **or** traffic)
4. When it goes into the country, the bus is _____.   (full **or** empty)
5. The bus goes back into the country to bring more _____ into town.   (goods **or** people)

More to think about

1. Write a sentence to answer each question.
    a) Does the bus route start in the town or in the country?
    b) Why do you think most people would be travelling?
    c) What lies between the country village and the town?
    d) Does the poem suggest whether it is a new or an old bus? How?

2. The poet uses some interesting descriptions.
   Copy into your book how he describes each of these.
    a) How the bus, full of passengers, goes up the hill.
    b) What the bus reminds us of as it forces its way through the traffic.
    c) How the bus seems happier to be out in the country again.
    d) What happens to the bus as it squeezes through tight spaces.
    e) How the passengers get onto the bus.

Now try these

1. In your book write ...
    a) something the conductor might have said when people were pushing and shoving to get onto the bus.
    b) something your mum, loaded with shopping, might have said when it started to rain as she was waiting for the bus, which was late.
    c) something you might have said when, one day, the bus was stuck in a snowdrift as you were on your way to school.

2. Write sentences to answer these questions.
   Sometimes machines, like Thomas the Tank Engine, can seem almost as though they are human.
    a) Do you think the poet thought this bus was like a person? Why?
    b) Do you have a machine, like a favourite toy or a bike, that seems to you to have a personality? Write about it.

UNIT 17
A Day When Frogs Wear Shoes

Julian, his best friend Gloria, and his little brother Huey, were sitting on the front steps of their house on a Caribbean island. It was a very hot day, and one of those days when they didn't know what to do.

My father has a workshop about a mile from our house, where he fixes cars. "Huey," I said, "usually, visiting Dad is a good idea. Today, it's a dangerous idea."
"Why?" Gloria said.
"Because we're bored," I said. "My dad hates it when people are bored. He says the world is so interesting nobody should ever be bored."
"So we'll go to see him," Huey said, "and we won't tell him we're bored. We're bored, but we won't tell him."
"Just you remember that!" I said.
"Oh, I'll remember," Huey said.
Huey was wearing an angel look. When he has that look, you know he'll never remember anything.
Huey and I put on sweat bands. Gloria put on dark glasses. We started out. The sun shone up at us from the pavements. Even the shadows on the street were hot as blankets.
Huey picked up a stick and scratched it along the pavement.
"Oh, we're bored," he muttered. "Bored, bored, bored, bored!"
"Huey!" I yelled. I wasn't bored any more. I was nervous.

Finally we reached a sign.
That's my Dad's sign.
My Dad is Ralph.
The car park had three cars in it.
Dad was inside the workshop,
lifting the bonnet of another car.
He didn't have any customers with him, so we didn't get to shake hands and feel like visiting mayors or VIPs.
"Hi, Dad," I said.
"Hi!" my Dad said.

RALPH'S CAR HOSPITAL
Punctures/Rust/Dents & Bashes
Bad Brakes   Bad Breaks
UNUSUAL COMPLAINTS

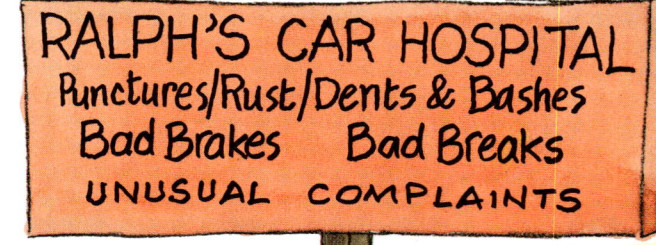

"We're —"
I didn't trust Huey. I stepped on his foot.
"We're on a hike," I said.
"I'm surprised at you kids picking a hot day like today for a hike," my father answered. "The ground is so hot. On a day like this, frogs wear shoes!"

Ann Cameron

Do you remember?

What words are missing?
Write them in your book.

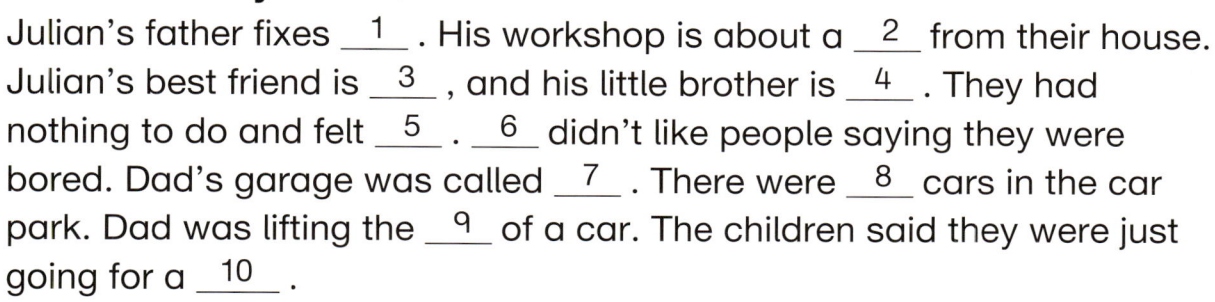

Julian's father fixes __1__ . His workshop is about a __2__ from their house. Julian's best friend is __3__ , and his little brother is __4__ . They had nothing to do and felt __5__ . __6__ didn't like people saying they were bored. Dad's garage was called __7__ . There were __8__ cars in the car park. Dad was lifting the __9__ of a car. The children said they were just going for a __10__ .

More to think about

Write a sentence to answer each question.
1. Where is the story set?
2. Why did Julian usually like visiting his father's workshop?
3. How do we know that Julian's father was a positive sort of person?
4. Why was Julian doubtful about going to the workshop on this day?
5. Why did they tell Ralph they were off on a hike?
6. How can we tell the weather was extremely hot?

Now try these

1. Write some sentences to describe these characters from the story. Think carefully before you start, and use the clues in the passage.
   a) Julian   b) Huey   c) Ralph, their dad
2. Think back to the hottest day you can remember. Write about where you were, what you were doing, and how you felt.

UNIT 18 Basilisks

Once upon a time, in a far off land, a strange thing happened, a very strange thing indeed. A cockerel laid an egg. Then, through the grass slithered a snake. The snake wrapped itself around the egg and kept it warm, and sure enough, after a time the shell began to crack. At this the snake quietly slithered away into the tall, dark grass.

From the broken shell emerged a strange and scary creature. It had the feet, body and wings of a cockerel, but the tail twisted and turned, and it had a long, forked, darting tongue. The head was that of a snake but the eyes were the protruding eyes of a toad.

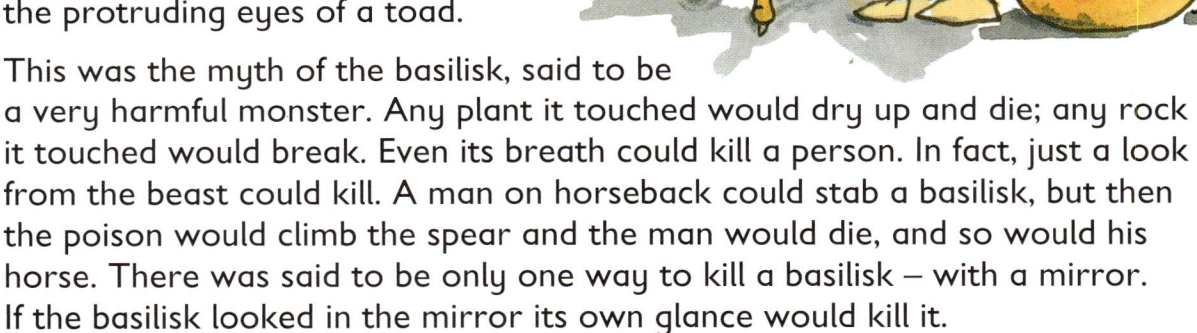

This was the myth of the basilisk, said to be a very harmful monster. Any plant it touched would dry up and die; any rock it touched would break. Even its breath could kill a person. In fact, just a look from the beast could kill. A man on horseback could stab a basilisk, but then the poison would climb the spear and the man would die, and so would his horse. There was said to be only one way to kill a basilisk – with a mirror. If the basilisk looked in the mirror its own glance would kill it.

People believed in basilisks for hundreds of years. In 1587 in Warsaw, Poland, two small girls were found dead in a cellar. Rumours circulated that a basilisk was to blame. Someone had an idea. There was a criminal about to be put to death for his crimes, so what did it matter if a basilisk killed him?

The criminal put on a leather suit, covered in mirrors, and went down into the cellar. When he emerged he was carrying something. At first it looked like a dead snake, but could it be a basilisk? Who knew? Few people had ever seen a real one, and those who had seen one had died. At last the king's doctor was called in. He studied the beast. "Yes," he said, "definitely a basilisk." The monster had struck again!

Do you remember?

1. Copy these sentences. Fill in the missing words.
   a) A _____ laid the egg.
   b) The egg was kept warm by a _____.
   c) The basilisk's body was like a _____.
   d) One part of the creature like a snake was its _____.
   e) The only way to kill a basilisk was with a _____.

2. Write a sentence to answer each question.
   a) Which part of the basilisk was like a toad?
   b) What happened if the basilisk breathed on you?
   c) Why couldn't a horseman kill the creature?
   d) Where were the two girls found dead?
   e) How did they eventually kill the basilisk in the cellar?

More to think about

1. Find the words or phrases in the passage that describe:
   a) how the snake moved
   b) the basilisk's tongue
   c) what the grass was like
   d) what the creature's eyes were like

2. The basilisk was said to have 'the protruding eyes of a toad'. Describe the eyes of three people or animals you know. Use good descriptive words.

Now try these

1. Write a few sentences describing the different feelings you would have had if you were the criminal told to kill the basilisk.

2. The myth of the basilisk is just one of hundreds of monster tales. Retell another monster tale in your book that you know, or make one up.

UNIT 19 Mrs Wobble the Waitress

Mrs Wobble, who keeps wobbling and dropping food, has been given the sack from the café where she worked.

"Cheer up, Ma!" they said.
"You will find another job in another café!"
But there were no other cafés.
That was the only one in town.
Mrs Wobble knew this.
"There are no other cafés," she said.
And she began to cry.
The children did not like to see their mother cry.
It made them cry.
It made their father cry too.
Then Mr Wobble had an idea.
"I know what we can do," he said.
"We can open a café of our own.
We can turn our house into a café!"
And they did...

The first customers arrived.
"Oh dear," said Mrs Wobble.
"What if I...?"
Mrs Wobble wobbled with a bowl of soup.
"Help!" said the customer.
Miss Wobble skated to the rescue.
She caught the soup in another bowl.
"That's clever!" the customer said.
Mrs Wobble wobbled with a roast chicken.
"Help!" said the customer.
Master Wobble skated to the rescue.
He caught the chicken in a net.
"Hooray!" the customer said.
Then all the customers cheered.
"This is more fun than a circus!" they said.

Allan and Janet Ahlberg

Do you remember?

Read these sentences about the story.
Copy only the ones that are true.
Mrs Wobble has been given the sack.
She is a bad cook.
She keeps dropping the food she is serving.
She is very upset.
She is pleased not to be working.
Mr Wobble suggests they open a café in their house.
Mrs Wobble doesn't wobble any more.
The Wobble children catch the food.
The customers think it is fun.

More to think about

1. Choose the words from each column to make sensible sentences.

Who?	Did what?	When?
Mrs Wobble	skated to the rescue	when she lost her job.
Mr Wobble	cheered	to catch the soup
Miss Wobble	had an idea	when he saw Mrs Wobble crying.
Master Wobble	was very upset	as they watched the excitement.
The customers	skated to the rescue	to catch the chicken.

2. Write a few sentences to tell how you think the story might finish. Try to make it interesting or funny.

3. Write a summary of the story of *Mrs Wobble the Waitress* in your own words. Try not to use more than 40 words.

Now try these

This is a funny story, but kitchens can be dangerous places.

1. Make a list of possible dangers in a kitchen.

2. Write a set of rules to help to make your kitchen at home a safer place.

3. Do you think writers should write funny stories about serious things? Give your reasons.

UNIT 20 Humans – friend or foe?

Sometimes people can befriend animals, but sometimes they can have very different intentions. Look carefully at this picture by the Indian artist Todi Ragini, and read this poem by an unknown Nigerian poet.

Kob Antelope

A creature to pet and
spoil like a child.
Smooth-skinned
stepping cautiously
in the lemon grass ...
The eyes
like a bird's.
The head
beautiful liked carved wood ...
Your neck seems long,
so very long
to the greedy hunter.

Anon (Yoroba)

Do you remember?

Write the correct answer to each question in your book.
1. Who painted the picture?
   a) The picture was painted by Todi Ragini, from India.
   b) The picture was painted by an unknown artist from Africa.

2. Who wrote the poem?
    a) The poem was written by Todi Ragini, from India.
    b) The poem was written by an unknown poet from Africa.
3. Is the woman in the picture a friend or an enemy of the creatures?
    a) The woman is a friend of the creatures.
    b) The woman is an enemy of the creatures.
4. Are the people in the poem kind to the animals?
    a) No, the poem is about people who want to hunt the animals.
    b) Yes, the poem is about people who want to help the animals.

More to think about

Write a sentence to answer each question.
1. Do you think the woman in the picture is poor or wealthy? How can you tell?
2. Why are the deer following her?
3. What is it about the animals that show they think they can trust the woman?
4. What words does the poet use to suggest that antelopes are shy creatures?
5. The poet compares the antelope's eyes to those of birds. What other similarities can you think of between deer and antelope and any other creatures?

Now try these

Deer hunting has been banned in some countries.
Do you think deer hunting is cruel and should be banned, or should hunters be allowed to hunt deer for food?
Write about what you think.

Progress Unit B: Being Angry

Here are two pieces of writing about being angry.

Not being allowed to watch his favourite TV programme makes Arthur very, very angry. And when Arthur really lets his temper fly, some astonishing things begin to happen...

"No," said his mother, "it's too late. Go to bed."
"I'll get angry," said Arthur.
"Get angry," said his mother.
So he did. Very, very angry.
He got so angry that his anger became
a stormcloud exploding thunder
and lightning and hailstones.
"That's enough," said his mother.
But it wasn't.
Arthur's anger became a hurricane
hurling rooftops and chimneys
and church spires.
"That's enough," said his father. But it wasn't.
Arthur's anger became a typhoon tipping whole towns into the seas.
"That's enough," said his grandfather. But it wasn't.
Arthur's anger became a universquake
and the earth and the moon
and the stars and the planets,
Arthur's country and Arthur's town, his street, his house, his garden
and his bedroom were nothing more than bits in space.
Arthur sat on a bit of Mars and thought.
He thought and thought.
"Why was I so angry?" he thought.
He never did remember.
Can you?

From *Angry Arthur* by Hiawyn Oram

Bertie Thomson won a prize for this poem when he was nine years old.

My Hair Black as Dirty Coal

My hair black as dirty coal,
My eyes sizzle like fried eggs in a pan,
My nose breathes heavily like a charging wild bull.
Because:

    (My brother...)

My mouth breathing fire like a dragon.
My stomach going in and out,
I clench my fists hard like compressing a lemon
until all the juice comes out.

    (kicked my...)

My anger bubbling inside,
Ready to fire out of my head.
I think I'm Arnold Schwarzenegger.
My feet heat up ready to kick out
And then I burst out.

    (ball over the fence!!)

Do you remember?

1. Think of sensible ways to finish each of these sentences about Arthur, and copy them into your book.
    a) Not being allowed to watch TV makes Arthur...
    b) His mother said...
    c) His anger was at first like...
    d) Then it became like a hurricane hurling...
    e) In the end he couldn't remember why...

2. Write a sentence to answer each question about Bertie.
    a) Who was he angry with?
    b) Why was he so cross?
    c) Which parts of his body did his anger affect?
    d) Did he manage to control his temper?

More to think about

1. Hiawyn Oram, the author of *Angry Arthur*, says Arthur's anger becomes other things. How can we tell that he is getting more and more angry as the story goes on?
2. Copy the similes Bertie uses to describe:
   a) how his eyes feel
   b) how his breathing is affected
   c) how he is holding his hands.
3. Which phrase tells us that in the end Bertie actually lost his temper?

Now try these

Write some sentences to answer these questions.

1. Do you think either Arthur or Bertie were right to feel as angry as they did? Why?
2. Do you feel sorry for Arthur or Bertie or both of them? Why?
3. Which of the two pieces of writing is the better description of someone getting really angry? Say why you think this.
4. Should we always try to control our anger, or should we sometimes allow ourselves to show our anger? Give reasons for your answer, and give some examples when it is probably better to control our feelings of anger.
5. Think of an occasion when you felt really angry.
   Why were you so cross? How did it make you feel?
   What happened in the end?